Maine: Year One

A photographic journal of a Southern
Californian's first year in the Pine Tree State.

Daniel B. Zukowski

Are You Crazy?

More than a year after moving from Southern California to Maine, I still get asked, "Are you crazy?" Well, that's for professionals to decide, but I do admit it seems odd to leave 72-and-sunny all year for below-zero winter days and the occasional Nor'easter.

I love California. I lived there for 25 years. The bulk of my career played out there. The endless coast, hikeable foothills, stark deserts and iconic mountains gave me many pleasures. I made and still cherish the many friends I have there. But it wasn't home.

Much of my family lives in the Northeast, where I grew up. Four seasons, hardwood forests and a different ocean make up my mental geography. But why Maine?

There are many beautiful places in the U.S., many great towns and cities, and many places where I would enjoy living. In Maine, the outdoors is a way of life. The Pine Tree State has 3,500 miles of coastline and deep-green forests. It's home to Acadia National Park and Mount Katahdin and Casco Bay. There's a vibrant arts community. Great foodie restaurants, craft beers and independent coffee shops abound.

One year on, I've found Mainers to be welcoming and friendly. I've made new friends and gotten involved in various activities. I'm walking, hiking and snowshoeing. My photography has been on exhibit in shows here, I'm writing more and have enjoyed opportunities to speak about my adventures. I'm more in touch with my family, which seems to mean more the older you get.

So I decided to put together this short book, a rather random journal of my first year here. If you live in Maine, or are thinking of doing so, or of visiting here, or have friends here, this might give you some glimpse into life here. And then you can decide if I'm crazy or not.

Daniel B. Zukowski
DBZphoto.com

Getting There

It never rains in Southern California, says the song lyric. So it was fitting that the afternoon I left Los Angeles, after the 53-foot semi had gobbled up my belongings, it poured. Serious deluge stuff. Eastbound traffic on the 10 freeway was at a crawl. The first 10 miles took a full hour. And I still had 3,400 more to go.

This powerful winter storm chased me across the continent. A planned six-day drive turned into eight. My route of choice had to be changed. Interstate 40 runs though high country in Northern Arizona and New Mexico, and blizzard conditions were forecast. It made sense to take the longer, more southerly route, following I-10 to Texas and then heading northeast on I-20 and I-30 to rejoin I-40. That would be my undoing.

My second night on the road - New Year's Eve - was spent at a roadside hotel in Las Cruces, New Mexico. I had crossed the Continental Divide at 4,585 feet under a blue-steel sky with cross-current winds whipping at the swaying tractor-trailers. By 9:00 a.m. the next day, I was heading east through El Paso, Texas. A dark gray roll cloud lingered over the foothills north of the city. By 10:30, the temperature had dropped to 29 degrees and rime ice was coating the grasses along the roadside.

The clouds lowered to dense fog, at times dropping visibility to just a few hundred feet. By the time I cut north on I-20, I was carefully making my way through a harrowing ice storm. I began to witness jackknifed trailer trucks on both sides of the road. One was on its side, another had its cab turned around, and yet another had its trailer split open with its load splashed out onto the median. Along a desolate 45-mile stretch of the highway, I counted 18 wrecked tractor-trailers.

Black ice and steep grades made a deadly combination. Twice I felt my car begin to slide, but I was able to keep it under control. By late afternoon, it was obvious that I wouldn't make my destination in Dallas and that the safe course would be to find a room for the night. I got off the highway in Odessa, and as the ice storm lingered, found myself there for two long days and nights.

I caught up to the storm again in Tennessee, where it rained, and then found snow as I headed north through Pennsylvania and across New England.

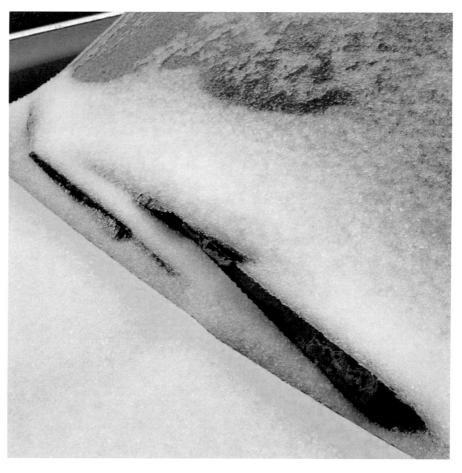

After two days iced-in at a hotel in Odessa, Texas, it took 30 minutes to unfreeze my car.

Blizzard

According to the University of Maine, the winter of 2015 "will be remembered as one of the harshest in Maine in recent decades." Thank you, and welcome to Maine.

There had already been a blizzard in November, well before I arrived in early January. Another major snowstorm on January 27 dropped nearly two feet of snow in Portland. That was followed by another blizzard on February 2, and that month was the state's coldest on record since 1895.

The piles of snow kept getting higher and higher. It seemed they were building Mount Everest right in my parking lot. Thankfully, Maine is prepared for snow, so roads were plowed quickly. Even the greenbelt path near my home would be cleared within a day or two after each snow, allowing me to go for long walks and stave off the winter drearies.

My car, which was always kept sparkling clean in California, was now hopelessly spattered in road muck and wore patches of snow and ice. A car wash lasted 15 minutes. For someone with pride-of-car, this was a major cultural adjustment.

The winter of 2014-2015 was the season when Boston broke all records with 110 inches of snow. Portland, Maine received 91 inches, some 50% more than its average of 62 inches. The city never went more than two days without snow between between January 24 and February 25. February saw 13 days with below-zero temperatures. Three inches of snow greeted the opening of the Portland Sea Dogs minor league baseball season on April 9, 2015.

No complaints. This is what I came for. All part of the adventure we call life.

The winter of 2014-2015 brought 90 inches of snow to coastal Maine, obliterating walkways and leaving no place to sit on this park bench.
This image was shot on film with a Holga 120N.

OVER: Portland Head Light, one of the most photographed lighthouses in New England, looks even prettier in winter.

Cities & Towns

I'm a nature photographer, so I don't spend a lot of time shooting in populated places. But I do usually have one of my cameras with me when I'm exploring a place, and I do enjoy walking in towns when I'm not out on the trail.

Maine's largest city is Portland, with about 67,000 residents, followed by Lewiston with 36,000. Lewiston and Auburn are twin cities divided by the Androscoggin River, and together they hold about 59,000 people. The capital is Augusta, with close to 19,000. Bangor is home to 32,500. That's a bit different from the 18.6 million population of Greater Los Angeles that I was used to.

I've yet to visit many of the cities, but I've come up with a few favorite places. Brunswick hosts Bowdoin College. Its eminently walkable campus with an eclectic architectural palette feels like a place to learn, and I enjoy visiting the Museum of Art and the Peary-MacMillan Arctic Museum.

Brunswick is just up the road from Freeport, home to L.L. Bean. The retailer's huge campus provides plenty of play space. The company holds events, lectures and outdoor activities on a regular basis. I've been privileged to speak there myself. Both Brunswick and Freeport boast excellent restaurants, as does Bar Harbor, the gateway to Acadia National Park.

There are many other interesting and enjoyable towns in Maine. I just haven't got to them yet. Perhaps that's for another book.

The twin towers of the 1855 Romanesque chapel on the campus of Bowdoin College in Brunswick, Maine rise 120 feet. On this cold March day, the gray stone is starkly set off by the clear, deep-blue sky.

Housed in a former church, Grace is now a restaurant in Portland.

Congress Street in Portland.

An original Wurlitzer juke box at a cafe in Bridgton.

Another cafe in Bridgton, which seems to be a colorful town.

On the Water

Maine boasts 3,500 miles of coastline and countless islands. Everyone knows of Maine lobsters, and the state's rich fishing tradition extends to herring, scallops and clams. Seafood is a way of life here.

My first encounter with Casco Bay was on a summer trip with a friend way back in 1975. I reacquainted myself with the Bay's islands and waters soon after I moved here. Casco Bay Lines offers numerous ferry and passenger boats to the major islands from Portland. Mostly, these provide transportation for seasonal and permanent residents of the islands, but are also popular with tourists and day-trippers. For just a few dollars, I can take a 15-minute ride out to Peaks Island and walk around for a few hours. Other, longer schedules allow you to catch sunrise or sunset out on the water.

Being on the water brings a sense of calm. I think it's something primal. The earth's surface is 71 percent water, and our bodies are about 60 percent water. Seems natural we'd be at home in it, or on it.

Popularly known as Bug Light, the Portland Breakwater Lighthouse stands guard over the entrance to Portland Harbor. A Casco Bay Lines ferry heads out to one of the numerous islands in the bay.

Fishing is an occupation, tradition, pleasure and the heritage of Maine.

A dory at rest in Casco Bay..

OVER: The summer sun sets over the Fore River as a seagull rests on pilings near Bug Light.

Lobster traps in Southwest Harbor.

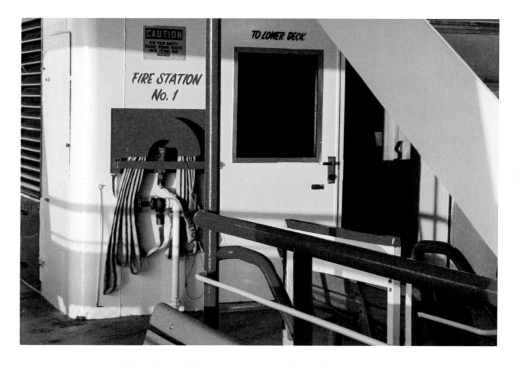

Aboard one of the Casco Bay Lines boats for a September
sunset cruise on Casco Bay.

OVER: Another view of Portland Head Light as the
morning sun peeks from behind the lighthouse.

On the Trail

I am a hiker. I hiked the Catskills and Shawangunks and Bear Mountain in Lower Hudson Valley when I was young. I've hiked in most of the Western states and Alaska. When my schedule allowed it, I'd be out three days a week in the foothills of Southern California.

So, naturally, when I came to Maine, the first thing I looked for was a trail map. There is an extensive network of state parks, nature preserves, and other public lands here. Maine Audubon, various and numerous land trusts, and some private holdings also open their properties to public use.

Maine is home to Acadia National Park and the Rachel Carson National Wildlife Refuge. Baxter State Park, which includes Mount Katahdin, encompasses more than 200,000 acres. Maine's 48 state parks cover beaches, lakes, rivers, forests and mountains. There are 50 miles of trails within Portland alone. There is no shortage of places to explore and no excuse for a sedentary existence here.

Both the Appalachian Mountain Club and the Maine Outdoor Adventure Club offer frequent outings for all skill levels, year-round. In addition to the physical health benefits of exercising your legs and lungs, spending time in nature has been shown to have positive mental health benefits. I couldn't agree more.

A forested trail in Wolfe's Neck State Park beckons in the dappled light of a warm June day.

A short trail and easy rock scramble lead to the beach at Wolfe's Neck State Park in Freeport. Across the short stretch of water is Googins Island, home to nesting ospreys each summer.

The tidal salt marsh of the Rachel Carson National Wildlife Refuge provides protected habitat for many birds including bald eagles and the endangered piping plover.

A portion of the Appalachian Trail passes the Grassy Pond area on its way to the top of Mount Katahdin in Baxter State Park. The lush greens are still evident one day before the autumnal equinox.

Mount Katahdin rises above Togue Pond in Baxter State Park.

Acadia National Park

The summit of Cadillac Mountain in Acadia National Park, where the first light of day shines on the Eastern seaboard, is invariably cold and windy despite its rather lowly elevation, mountain-wise, of 1,530 feet. At least, that has been my experience.

It can also be crowded, especially in the summer, and especially at sunrise and sunset. The park road leading up Cadillac Mountain has been known to achieve gridlock status at times in July and August. It is a magnificent view, but there are plenty of other great features within this park.

Acadia was the first national park in the East, and was established the same year as the National Park Service, 1916. One of this park's most endearing features is its 45 miles of carriage roads, a gift of John D. Rockefeller, that can be hiked in summer and skied or snowshoed in winter. Bicycles are also permitted on many sections. Sixteen feet wide and formed of broken stone, these roads rise and fall gently. Seventeen stone bridges are visual hallmarks of the carriage roads.

I've adopted Acadia as my home park, and have enjoyed hiking around Jordan Pond, Eagle Lake, the Sieur de Monts area and Sand Beach. White-tailed deer are occasionally seen, and peregrine falcons can be observed from the Precipice trailhead from mid-April to August.

Autumn is spectacular in Acadia. The mountains come alive with color and the trails overhang with brilliant reds and yellows. Cruise ships stop in nearby Bar Harbor to enable passengers to tour the park and see the multihued fall colors. Winter is soft and quiet, while spring brings warmth and renewal to Mount Desert Island.

One of the many scenic stone bridges that carry 45 miles of carriage roads as they meander through Acadia National Park.

OVER: Champlain Mountain is reflected in a lush beaver pond along Schooner Head Road in spring. When I went back here in the fall, the pond had dried up and this scene no longer existed.

The foggy and rocky coast of Maine on Mount Desert Island,
looking toward Otter Cliff.

Sand Beach on a clear, sunny October morning.

Fall foliage comes to rest in shallow waters along the Hadlock Pond loop.

OVER: At 5:55 p.m. on October 20, 2015, atop the summit of Cadillac Mountain, the sky blazes orange as the sun has just set.

Roads & Rails

Give me a road to drive, a train to ride or a plane to fly. Any one of these will take you to new places and new experiences. Travel widens your horizons. And besides that, I just enjoy it.

Maine's scenic roads will take you up the coast, around the state's many lakes and into the mountains. Route 1 is among the nation's oldest highways, connecting many of Maine's major cities and rambling through its quaintest towns. Route 15 runs from way up in northwest Maine, down along Moosehead Lake, through Bangor and ending on the coast at Deer Isle. Route 11 begins at the Canadian border at Fort Kent and heads down through Aroostook County to Millinockett, which serves as the gateway to Baxter State Park and Mount Katahdin - the northern terminus of the Appalachian Trail.

As for trains, Maine has only one Amtrak service connecting Brunswick and Portland with Boston. But the state has had the foresight to hold and preserve abandoned rail lines, with the potential for bringing them back to life someday for freight or passenger service.

Much rail history has been preserved in Maine. Once flush with narrow gauge logging railroads, portions of these are in operation now as tourist railroads and museums.

We lost one passenger train at the end of 2015. A private operator, the Maine Eastern Railroad, which had run seasonal trains from Brunswick to Rockland for 12 years, lost a bid to continue operating the line, and the new operator was unwilling to continue the passenger train. I documented the last regularly-scheduled runs and rode the last train.

But, our roads and rails connect with the rest of the nation that lies west and mostly south of our state, and I'll be on those trains and driving those highways.

The watchful engineer keeps a hand on the throttle of this historic narrow gauge steam locomotive on the Wiscasset, Waterville & Farmington Railway.

The curving Casco Bay Bridge glistens in the morning sunlight. This important structure connects Portland and South Portland across the Fore River.

PRECEDING PANEL: On one of its last runs, the Maine Eastern Railroad's passenger train approaches Newcastle amid a classic New England fall landscape.

Lowe's Bridge, near Guilford, was constructed in 1990 patterned after the original 1857 covered bridge over the Piscataquis River on this site.

*Somesville is the oldest settlement on Mount Desert Island, dating from 1781.
Its historic footbridge is reflected in the waters of Somes Pond on a fall day.*

Lightning Source UK Ltd.
Milton Keynes UK
UKRC021139101019
351329UK00005B/138